Amar'e Stoudemire

by Michael Sandler

Consultant: Charlie Zegers
Basketball Expert
basketball.about.com

BEARPORT
PUBLISHING

New York, New York

Credits

Cover and Title Page, © Ray Amati/NBAE via Getty Images, © Barry Gossage/NBAE via Getty Images, and © Mariela Lombard/ZUMA Press/Newscom; 4, © AP Photo/Jacquelyn Martin; 5, © Nathaniel S. Butler/NBAE via Getty Images; 7T, © Barry Gossage/NBAE via Getty Images; 7B, © Gary W. Green/KRT/Newscom; 8, © Linda Spillers/WireImage/Getty Images; 9L, © Linda Spillers/WireImage/Getty Images; 10, © Gary I. Rothstein/Icon SMI/Newscom; 11, © Barry Gossage/NBAE via Getty Images; 12, © E.A. Ornelas/San Antonio Express/ZUMA Press/Newscom; 13, © Christian Petersen/Getty Images; 14, © Wenzelberg/Splash News/Newscom; 15, © CJ Gunther/EPA/Landov; 16, © Mariela Lombard/ZUMA Press/Newscom; 17, © Courtesy of Praters Athletic Flooring/pratersathleticflooring.com; 18, © Giacomo Pirozzi/Panos; 19, © AP Photo/Steve Nesius; 20, © AP Photo/Frank Franklin II; 21, © AP Photo/Kathy Kmonicek; 22R, © Stephane Reix/For Picture/Corbis; 22L, © MCT/Newscom.

Publisher: Kenn Goin
Senior Editor: Lisa Wiseman
Creative Director: Spencer Brinker
Photo Researcher: We Research Pictures, LLC

Library of Congress Cataloging-in-Publication Data

Sandler, Michael, 1965–
   Amar'e Stoudemire / by Michael Sandler ; consultant, Charlie Zegers.
      p. cm. — (Basketball Heroes Making a Difference)
   Includes bibliographical references and index.
   ISBN 978-1-61772-442-8 (library binding) — ISBN 1-61772-442-4 (library binding)
   1. Stoudemire, Amar'e. 2. Basketball players—United States—Biography-—Juvenile literature.
3. African American basketball players—Biography—Juvenile literature. 4. Generosity—Juvenile
literature. I. Zegers, Charlie. II. Title.
   GV884.S38A3 2012
   796.323092—dc23
   [B]
                                    2011043247

For more information, write to Bearport Publishing Company, Inc., 45 West 21st Street, Suite 3B, New York, New York 10010. Printed in the United States of America.

10 9 8 7 6 5 4 3 2 1

Contents

Amazing Amar'e

As the last seconds ticked down on the clock during the game against the Denver Nuggets on December 12, 2010, New York Knicks fans rose from their seats to cheer. Their hero, power **forward** Amar'e Stoudemire, had done it again, scoring 30 points or more for the eighth straight game! More important, Amar'e had led the Knicks to an eighth straight win, a 129–125 defeat against the Nuggets.

Late in the game when it really counted, Amar'e had been amazing. During one third-quarter stretch, he scored 12 **consecutive** points. He hit a short **jumper**, two perfect free throws, a **layup**, a monstrous slam dunk, and two more jump shots to finish the 12-point run. Then in the fourth quarter, he hit five more shots. After the win, Amar'e talked excitedly about his team's potential. "The sky's the limit," he said.

Amar'e joined the New York Knicks in the 2010–2011 season and quickly became a fan favorite.

The win over the Nuggets on December 12, 2010, was also the New York Knicks' 13th victory in 14 games. Here, Amar'e (right) shoots against the Nuggets.

Amar'e Stoudemire's eight straight games with 30 or more points set a new Knicks record.

A Father's Words

"The sky's the limit" are words that Amar'e had once heard directed at him. They were the last words his father, Hazell, had said to him before he died of a heart attack when Amar'e was just 12 years old.

While Hazell had great confidence in his son's **potential**, achieving it would be a struggle for young Amar'e. His father's death was just one difficulty he had to overcome while growing up in central Florida. For example, Amar'e's family was very poor and they lived in a neighborhood filled with crime and drugs. His mother and his older brother were often in trouble with the law. After his father's death, Amar'e bounced around from home to home. Sometimes he lived with his basketball coaches while his mother was in prison.

Amar'e didn't play much basketball as a small child. His father was a football coach, and football was Amar'e's favorite sport. He didn't play organized basketball until eighth grade.

A 21-year-old Amar'e poses for a photo with his mother.

Amar'e (right) with his younger brother Marwan

A Place of Peace

During Amar'e's teen years, he faced many challenges at school as well as at home. Though Amar'e had been a good elementary school student, his grades suffered after his father's death. Switching schools because of his frequent moves didn't help either. Amar'e attended six different schools in four years. There was one place, however, where Amar'e never felt troubled—on the basketball court.

At age 14, Amar'e discovered that basketball was his sport. At six feet six (1.98 m), he was both tall and incredibly talented. "I knew I was good," he said, "because I was the only 14-year-old who could dunk backward."

The game was always a welcome escape from his difficult life. "On the court," said one of his youth coaches, "he was just in another world. He would be at peace."

Amar'e shoots the ball during the 2002 Jordan Brand Capital Classic, the oldest national high school all-star basketball game in the country.

While in high school, Amar'e (left) was named Most Valuable Player during the 2002 Jordan Brand Capital Classic.

Since he was a teenager, Amar'e has been nicknamed STAT. The letters stand for "Standing Tall and Talented."

From High School to the NBA

Since Amar'e moved around so much and attended many different schools, he was barely able to play two full seasons of high school basketball. Still, in that short time, he established himself as the country's most explosive high school player. He was an amazing leaper, a ferocious dunker, a scary shot blocker, and a powerful **rebounder**. In his senior year at Cypress Creek High School in Orlando, he was named Florida's Mr. Basketball. This award is given to the state's single best player.

After graduating from high school, Amar'e made a choice. Instead of going to college, he wanted to head straight to the NBA. He wanted to start earning money to help out his struggling family. He felt he was ready to play at basketball's highest level. The sky's the limit, his father had told him—and Amar'e was ready to see if that was really true!

In his senior high school season, Amar'e averaged 29 points, 15 rebounds, and 6 blocks a game.

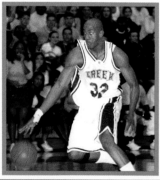

Amar'e entered the 2002 NBA **draft** and was chosen ninth by the Phoenix Suns. He was the only player straight out of high school selected that year.

Amar'e talks to reporters after being drafted by the Phoenix Suns.

The Sensational Suns

After being drafted by the Suns, reporters asked Amar'e how he felt about going up against **veteran All-Stars** such as Kevin Garnett and Tim Duncan. The young **rookie** replied that he had no fear. "I've already faced tough situations," he said. "This is a piece of cake."

Amar'e backed up his words with his actions. In his first season, he averaged more than 13 points and 8 rebounds a game, becoming the first player to earn the Rookie of the Year Award straight out of high school. The next season, he increased his scoring to more than 20 points a game, and was selected to play for the U.S. Olympic team.

In 2004–2005, **point guard** Steve Nash joined the Suns. For the next six seasons, six-feet-three (1.91-m) Steve and six-feet-ten (2.08-m) Amar'e became the most feared small man–big man combination in basketball. The pair led Phoenix to five playoff appearances, including three trips to the **Western Conference** Finals. With all this success, it seemed that the sky was the only limit for Amar'e!

"I never had a doubt that I would make it to the NBA," said Amar'e. "I always stayed focused because my family was going bad, and I wanted to be able to take care of them."

Amar'e (left) and Steve Nash (right) during a game in 2010

While playing for the Suns, Amar'e overcame serious injuries. He missed much of the 2005–2006 season due to knee surgery. The goggles that he wears today are to protect his eyes after he required eye surgery in 2009. After each injury, Amar'e has bounced back to be just as strong as he was before he was hurt!

New Challenge in New York

After eight years in Phoenix, Amar'e decided he was ready to play for a new team. Before the 2010–2011 season, he signed with the New York Knicks as a **free agent**. The troubled Knicks had won only 29 games the previous season. They hadn't made the playoffs in seven years. Amar'e looked forward to helping the team bounce back. No other superstar except Amar'e was willing to take on this challenge.

Showing no fear, Amar'e quickly turned the Knicks around. He became the team's high scorer and on-court leader. His eight-game scoring streak turned Knicks fans into **fanatics**. Their excitement grew even stronger when he led the once hopeless team into the 2010–2011 playoffs.

Amar'e wearing a New York Knicks hat in front of Madison Square Garden, the Knicks' home arena

Amar'e (left) tries to keep the ball away from Kevin Garnett during the 2010–2011 playoff series against the Boston Celtics.

Amar'e was injured during the Knicks' 2010–2011 playoff series against the Boston Celtics. The Celtics won the series, 4–0.

Overcoming Difficulties

Today, even as an NBA All-Star, Amar'e remembers how tough life can be. That's why he works so hard to help others, especially children, who are facing difficulties. In order to provide a helping hand, he started a **charity** in 2003 called the Amar'e Stoudemire Foundation.

First focusing on kids in Phoenix, and later in New York, the group tries to help children beat **poverty** by supporting their education. The foundation provides school supplies and educational opportunities to kids who really need them. In Phoenix, for example, Amar'e opened a reading and learning center for local children. He also visited schools to inspire kids to learn.

Education is especially important to Amar'e because as a teenager, he had no one to give him guidance. "I had nobody to force education on me," Amar'e said. "I feel like if I could do it all over again, I'd definitely be a nerd."

Amar'e visits with a group of kids to talk about the importance of going to school and getting a good education.

The new basketball court at the
Taylor-Wythe Community Center

In March 2011, Amar'e helped open a new
basketball court at the Taylor-Wythe Community
Center in Brooklyn, New York. Basketball had
helped Amar'e stay out of trouble when he was
growing up. "I hope I can do the same thing for
kids in Brooklyn," he said.

Aiming for Africa

In addition to helping kids who live in the United States, Amar'e is also focused on making a difference in the lives of people in Africa. In some African countries, people struggle to get basic necessities, such as food and water. In 2008, Amar'e traveled to Sierra Leone, a country where many people don't have clean drinking water and often get sick from drinking polluted water. Being sick can make it impossible for children to attend school on a regular basis. To help these people, Amar'e and his foundation build **wells** that produce clean water. "One water well built provides water for 450 people," said Amar'e.

Amar'e is also helping teens in Africa learn to play and excel at the game he loves. His foundation has worked in the country of Mali to teach basketball skills, pay for basketball camps and tournaments, and give young players **scholarships** to come to the United States for basketball skill training.

Amar'e helped build wells similar to this one in Sierra Leone.

A court at the IMG
Basketball Academy

One basketball player in Mali who Amar'e has helped is 16-year-old Boubacar Moungoro. Amar'e's foundation paid for Boubacar to fly from Mali to Florida to live and train at the IMG Basketball Academy.

No Time to Lose

Sometimes it seems like STAT is in a hurry. He couldn't wait to help his family. He couldn't wait to reach the NBA. Today, he can't wait to help bring a championship to his new team, the New York Knicks. He loves being in New York. "The fans are incredible," he said, and he wants to reward them with a **title** as soon as possible.

He is just as impatient about making a difference in the lives of others. He visits schools. He travels to far-away countries. He's always reading, trying to learn more about the world, and finding ways he can help less fortunate people.

Why is he in such a hurry? Amar'e knows that when it comes to basketball success or helping others improve their lives, there is no reason not to try to do as much as you possibly can. The sky is the only limit on what one can do.

Amar'e (right) shoots against Andrew Bogut of the Milwaukee Bucks in 2010.

Amar'e is a spokesperson for the UNICEF Believe in Zero campaign, which is trying to reduce the number of children who die each day from **preventable diseases** from 25,000 to zero.

The Amar'e File

Amar'e is a basketball hero on and off the court. Here are some highlights.

● Amar'e played in his first All-Star Game in 2005, the first of six trips in his career. When Amar'e was voted onto the Eastern Conference All-Star team as a **starter** in 2011, he became the first New York Knick to receive that honor since **center** Patrick Ewing in 1997.

● When he retires from basketball, Amar'e has said that he would like to become a teacher, something he dreamed about as a kid.

● The player nicknamed STAT has put up some incredible **statistics** since joining the NBA. In his rookie year, STAT scored 38 points in a game against the Minnesota Timberwolves, a record for rookies coming straight out of high school. His career high is 50 points, set against the Portland Trail Blazers in 2005.

Glossary

All-Stars (AWL-starz) players chosen to compete in games in which the best NBA players from the Eastern Conference play against the best NBA players from the Western Conference

center (SEN-tur) one of the standard positions on a basketball team, usually played by the tallest player

charity (CHA-ruh-tee) a group that tries to help people in need

consecutive (kuhn-SEK-yuh-tiv) happening one after the other

draft (DRAFT) an event in which professional teams take turns choosing college athletes to play for them

fanatics (fuh-NAT-iks) people who care very strongly about something

forward (FOR-wurd) one of the standard positions on a basketball team that is often responsible for much of the team's scoring; a team's two forwards are generally taller than the guards but shorter than the team's center

free agent (FREE AY-juhnt) a player who no longer has a contract with a team and is free to join any team

jumper (JUHMP-ur) a jump shot; a shot taken by a player while jumping

layup (LAY-uhp) a shot taken near the basket, usually by playing the ball off the backboard

point guard (POINT GARD) the basketball player whose main jobs are to run plays and pass the ball to teammates who are in a position to score

potential (puh-ten-shuhl) what a person is capable of achieving

poverty (POV-ur-tee) being very poor

preventable diseases (pri-VENT-ay-buhl duh-ZEEZ-iz) diseases that can be avoided, for example, by vaccines

rebounder (REE-bown-dur) a player who catches a ball off of the basket after a missed shot

rookie (RUK-ee) a first-year player

scholarships (SKOL-ur-ships) grants of money given to people for education

starter (START-ur) a person who plays at the start of a game; the best player at a position

statistics (stuh-TISS-tiks) numbers that show how well a player does

title (TYE-tuhl) championship

veteran (VET-ur-uhn) a player with a lot of experience

wells (WELZ) deep holes dug in the ground to get water

Western Conference (WESS-turn KON-fur-*uhnss*) one of two 15-team divisions making up the NBA

Bibliography

Anderson, Kelli. "Raising Arizona." *Sports Illustrated* (January 20, 2003).

Ganguli, Tania. "Stoudemire Stepping It Up On and Off the Court." *Standard-Examiner* (October 1, 2009).

Jenkins, Lee. "The Savior Cometh." *Sports Illustrated* (February 14, 2011).

Peterson, Rob. "The Amar'e of One." *Hoop Magazine* (March/April 2011).

Read More

Frisch, Aaron. *New York Knicks (NBA Champions).* Mankato, MN: Creative Company (2008).

Knobel, Andy. *New York Knicks (Inside the NBA).* Mankato, MN: ABDO (2012).

Learn More Online

To learn more about Amar'e Stoudemire and the New York Knicks, visit
www.bearportpublishing.com/BasketballHeroes

Index